Revealed to be Healed

Own It on the Journey

Paula Carroll

Copyright © 2018 Paula Carroll

All rights reserved.

ISBN:1719164762
ISBN-13:9781719164764

TABLE OF CONTENTS

Acknowledgments	ii
Introduction	5
Owning	7
The Little Girl of my Past	9
My Health Journey	14
Broken Relationship Journey	19
Reflection	25
What to do to Move On	29
The Stop Signs	35
Reflection	41
Accept the Following to Move On	44
Reflection	47
Release It	51
Reflection	57
Using It	61
Reflection	67
About the Author	71

Revealed to Be Healed

DEDICATION

I dedicate this book to the women who motivate and inspire me to be who I am today. No matter how difficult life got for me on my journey, God always placed a group of women to help me along the journey. From my grandmother, mother, aunt Alda, twin sister Paulette and nieces, to my sista friend Althea Bates, church sistas from Rehoboth Church of God and Ebenezer Church of God, and spiritual leaders-Sis Nessa and Rev. Porter Cox. I would not be the person I am today if I did not have this network of women in my life touching a part of my journey in one way or another.

Revealed to be Healed   Paula Carroll

ACKNOWLEDGMENTS

I would like to first acknowledge the Lord Jesus Christ, my Savior. Thank you for never giving up on me, Lord.

I would like to acknowledge my mother who has been my biggest supporter, my sisters and nieces who saw me through the worst and just know how to make me laugh and allow me to just be myself.

I would like to acknowledge the sistas of SISTAS JOURNEY who joined and shared their own story on the journey. Thank you for your support and dedication.

Rev. Porter Cox, I acknowledge you for being a teacher, mentor, counselor and spiritual leader. I truly appreciate you.

Dr. Jackie Evans Phillips, I acknowledge you for seeing the writer in me. Thank you for believing in me and giving me the opportunity to put my story on paper.

Revealed to be Healed   Paula Carroll

Introduction

Life is a journey and everyone faces a particular story on the journey that was difficult. Even though that story on the journey brought hurt, gave you pain, made you feel fearful, disappointed and even ashamed, there is purpose for it all. In the ears of others, that story you are in may sound crazy, unbelievable, and may be even out of the norm. In the midst of *my* story, I heard the spirit of God telling me, "You need to own it. You need to release it and watch how I, God, will use it for the good."

Revealed to Be Healed-Owning It on the Journey is written with the intention of helping you own that story and seek to build resiliency as overcomers. No one is an Island and every journey in life requires the support of someone else. Life's journey comes in many facets and is packaged in three main factors: Physical, Emotional, and Spiritual. When one or more of these are weakened or even broken, there is a need for healing. Unfortunately, sometimes the healing process is delayed because the process of owning it has not been realized.

Revealed to Be Healed-Owning It on the Journey contains steps in owning, releasing, and using your story, Bible verses to encourage you on the journey, and personal prayers prayed on the journey. This book will help you celebrate the journey you are on. Each page will allow you to see that each story on the journey is a part of who you are today and that is worth celebrating. As you read, you will be able to reflect and draw on your own journey and express in writing on the spaces provided at the end of the chapter. The Journey continues and there are more stories to be unfolded. Let this book help you own where you are and who you are on the journey.

Own It & Be Healed!!

Owning it

I am a sista on a Journey. This is my story, my life. On my journey, I had to make choices. Sometimes I made good choices and there were other times when I made some not so good ones. I had some accomplishments and good days but there were some times when I was broken, down, and felt like a failure. But, through it all, my story on the journey is mine; it is who I am and it keeps evolving as I continue to journey in this life.

I remember as a young girl, my journey was full of self-doubt. I did not think I could accomplish much. Low self-esteem and procrastination were my best friends. I was this shy and quiet girl who did not like her body image; even the sound of my voice disgusted me. I brought all these negative feelings of myself into my adulthood. On the outside, I painted a picture of a person who was always happy and nothing affected her. But the truth was, things did affect me and I wasn't always happy.

I allowed myself to enjoy the accomplishments I made openly but cried inwardly over the brokenness of my life. Inside, I was beating up myself and lived in hurt, disappointments, and shame for all the mistakes I made and the bad decisions I made. From getting pregnant at age 14, not knowing how to express myself, choosing wrong relationships, reaching 40 and feeling unaccomplished, dealing with reproductive issues that led to being childless to trying to hold on to a broken marriage, these are some of the things I tried to bury inside me, wishing they weren't a part of my story.

> Sometimes, I don't understand your leading Lord but I will trust you anyhow. Sometimes I am confused in the midst of my situation; but I know you are Lord and you are working it out. Lord, you are victorious so with you I find victory. I trust and believe you God. Amen.

We may not agree with the people in our life but having mutual respect for each is something I learned and value.

The Little Girl of my Past

I am the firstborn of twins and the quiet one (at least, in my opinion). I am the third born of the five children my mother has, four of whom are girls. My dad has nine children, seven of whom are girls.

I was that little girl who longed to have her father in her life. I wanted my dad to be more than that dad we visited sometimes and the man my mother had to fight for child maintenance. Growing up, I could not understand why my mother and father could not be together like in my dreams. Then my mother shared with me and my sisters some of the behaviors of my dad and even then I didn't want to own the truth. It was easier to dream of the life I wanted than to own the truth.

One thing I have learned from my mother and father and that is the value of friendship. Despite the struggles they endured with each other, they stayed great friends, even now. I will forever be grateful for that lesson. We may not agree with the people in our life, but having mutual respect for each is something I learned and value.

I can remember, as a little girl, struggling with pronouncing my words and that contributed to my being a quiet child. 'Introvert' is the word I learned later in life that describes my personality. It was only later in my life that I was able to come to term with being an introvert and even accepting it as part of my journey. So, when I go back in my mind to who I was as a little girl, I realize I did not like me very much and I rarely spoke my mind.

I was skinny with long legs, thick lips, big eyes, and had a voice I did not like. I was quiet and only spoke when someone talked to me. In class, if the teacher did not call on me, it was like I wasn't there. My twin sister was, in my eyes, more popular and outspoken than I was. I had friends but not as many as she did.

As I developed into a teen, liking me became even more difficult. My legs seemed to have grown longer, my eyes bigger, and that voice! And, guess what? I now had breasts. I noticed they were bigger than my sister's at the time. Boy, did I feel like an ugly duckling. I did not think boys would like me so, of course, as soon as a boy seemed to be looking my way, it was like heaven. I wanted to be noticed by boys so bad. As a teen, I didn't think boys really liked me as a person except for the fact that I was a girl. When a boy brought up sex to me, I just thought that was what boys do with girls they like, not realizing I was just one of the girls these boys "like."

At age fourteen, I met this guy who was older, and he expressed much interest in me. We talked a lot and I thought he liked me, so sex became the thing we did. By the time my fifteenth birthday came around, I found out that I was pregnant. I went into denial and was wishing it would just be a bad dream that would end. I hid it from my mother and sisters but before long people started talking. I was threatened with abortion and then I was sent away for a short time. Eventually, my mother took me back.

Throughout the pregnancy, all I can remember is feeling ashamed and disappointed. This was a very confusing part of my journey, especially when I gave birth and my son died three days after he was born. Did I tell you the father did stick around and own up to the pregnancy? Yes, he did. It was his first child as well.

I became very angry with God because something I was wishing for did not happen and hoping it just disappeared became real and then I gave birth and the child just died. No explanation was given to me as to why he died. So much pain; so much to deal with at such a young age. All I wanted at that time was to go back to the innocent years: the years when all I did was play with dolls, ramp and play house with my sisters and didn't have to think about 'grown people' business.

This part of my journey, I wasn't proud of and felt that I was a failure to myself and to my family. My family and the people around me now treated me differently. I was now talked about. I was now the girl who had got pregnant, and the baby died. I wanted so much to prove to everyone I could do better. I wanted so much to do my life all over again. I was still the quiet girl so all that I was suffering inside and outside I just did what I am told and smiled a lot, making sure I didn't disappoint anyone.

Revealed to be Healed — Paula Carroll

At age sixteen, I migrated to the US and all I wanted to do was prove to myself and to others that I could do better. I focused on being a good student, kept my feelings to myself, and not disappointing my family. I completed high school and went to college. I thought maybe now they would not see me as the girl who had got pregnant and who had lost the baby. For years, I tried to not accept this part of my journey and for years I did not want anyone to know I had given birth to a son at age fifteen.

This little girl grew up to be an adult, still quiet, struggling with expressing my feelings. I had big dreams but became best friends with procrastination. I continued to show people I was happy even when I was not. My goal after being a teen mom and traveling to the US was to go to college and that I did. I am proud of this accomplishment but kept thinking I can do so much more.

I enjoyed my college years but remember dealing with depression and the feeling I should be doing more. I remember after changing my major and preparing for graduation only to find out at my last advisory meeting that I would not be able to graduate on time because I was missing some credits. I was so disappointed. I thought to myself, "here I go again. I am letting down my family yet again." It took a while before I realized I would have to accept what was happening. I finally let my family know I would not graduate as planned and that I must do another semester. I was working so hard not to disappoint anyone that I forgot what I wanted for me.

I completed college over the summer and graduated December of that year. Yes, I felt good to have accomplished my goal of going to college and completing but still felt unaccomplished. I still felt I didn't do my best and was still disappointed I had to graduate in December. All those feelings I kept inside and did not share.

> At my road block, God, I stand still, hold onto you and wait for you to move. When you move, God, I move because my help comes from you, God. I leave my past and move forward with God. Amen.

My Health Journey

College grad, living in my own place, have a good job – At age 27, I am feeling like I am ok. Not all that I want in life but Ok. Then, this part of my **Journey** was about to be hit with an unpredictable health crisis. My menstrual cycle has always been an issue for me since my late teens into my twenties. But, like most women, I brushed it off and said, "I just must deal with it." The rocking myself to sleep, eating painkillers, changing pads every hour, calling out of work because the flow is so heavy, all of this I was thinking was normal for women.

Then the pain got worse. Now, it is not just cramps, it is also back pain, right shoulder and chest pain. I kept saying, "it is just bad cramps. It's just bad period!" Until the chest pain got worse and I began throwing up. I could hardly breathe without pain.

"What is this?" I ask.

But I was still thinking, *it's just bad cramps*. I was at work and throwing up. My friend shared a joke and I couldn't laugh. I finally realized I must go to the hospital and that I did. After x-rays and talking to several doctors, I ended up laying in a hospital bed with a chest tube hanging from my chest. Three weeks passed and doctors couldn't tell me what was wrong with me.

After four weeks in the hospital, the result of the biopsy of blood coming from my chest showed I have *endometriosis* in my lungs.

Endometriosis? This was my first time hearing the word. *What is it?* I think to myself. How long did I have this and how did I get it? I did not have much information to go on. When I was in my early 20s in college, I remember having the same symptoms. I was in so much pain as I was going to class. I had made my way to the nurse's office with chest pain and difficulty breathing. The ambulance came and brought me to the hospital where I was told it may have been a ruptured fibroid. So *endometriosi*s was very strange to me.

Let me pause here and tell you about an amazing thing that happened during my health story. You remember the only time I mentioned God in my childhood journey was when I said I was angry with Him when I had lost my son? Well, I must share that my mother and grandmother had made sure church was a part of our life growing up. I used to sing on the choir (I can't sing), I was in all the church plays and was in Sunday School early Sunday mornings. Since I became a pregnant fifteen year old girl, God went to the back burner on my journey. But, even though I put God on the back-burner, God did not put me away. He was right there working things out-I came to understand later in life.

You see, God had placed some people in my life right before my health crisis happened that would be there for me during the crisis. In my work environment, I was surrounded with people who cared about me. By the time that crisis hit, I had people praying for me, both family and friends. I started to see God in a different light.

I had not been a part of a church since I left Jamaica. After college, the club scene was my weekend ritual. Like clockwork, you could find me in the club weekend after weekend. During the time I was dealing with a collapsed lung and did not know what was going to happen to me, I was invited to church by my very good friend Althea and her mom Sis Nessa and they became my spiritual family.

The day I went to church was the first in many years. I had a chest tube hanging from my chest at that time and sitting up was very uncomfortable. I remember the altar call for those needing prayer. I knew about God's healing power, so I went to the altar for healing. As I stood at the altar, I started to think about the healer and realized it would be hard to ask for healing and not accept the healer. By the time the altar worker came to me, I was ready and willingly confessed my sins and accepted Jesus as my Lord and Savior. I just could not leave that altar without Jesus.

Today, I can say I have done many things since that day, but I have not let go of Jesus since that day I accepted Him, and He has not let go of me. In less than one week from that Sunday, I underwent two experimental surgeries in the attempt to repair my lungs. The doctor explained to me that they had to seal my lung to my chest wall. At that time, I was one of 100 people in the US to have *endometriosis* attacking organs outside of the uterus. Doctors from UConn Medical Center came to talk to me due to how rare this condition was.

My Health crisis did not end there because I learned later that *endometriosis* was a disease of the uterus and I had to undergo more surgeries to remove *endometriosis* and fibroids. It was then the doctor told me I will have difficulty getting pregnant. I was told I may have to have an egg donor if I wanted to get pregnant. I was on and off the medication such as *Depo Lupron* which shut my system down and I had experienced pre-menopause. I could not believe I would be discussing menopause symptoms with my mother who was at the age to go through it. I prayed God will skip me when I reach the right age later in life.

In November 2011, I counted 5 surgeries I had and, at that time, I was recovering from a surgery to remove uterine fibroids. I thought to myself, *this is it. I can't do another surgery.* I wish I could say that was it. In July 2016, I was told I may have to do a hysterectomy due to several growing fibroids. This hit me hard. God knows I wanted to have a baby. I am now in my early 40s but I have hopes for a child.

I was able to talk to another doctor who explained two options for surgery. I chose the myomectomy and explained to my doctor my hope of having a child and that I wanted her to save my uterus. Only if medically necessary should they take anything other than the fibroids. In February 2017, I had the surgery and found out the doctors removed ten fibroids. The recovery was painful but, with God, I was able to pull through. To date, I had two IVF and at early 40's, no child. But, can I tell you that journey is not ended until God says so. I still believe in miracles and that too I must own on the journey.

> My God will fight my battle. I will draw closer to my God. He will give me clear direction and my tongue will proclaim your righteousness, your praise all day long. Amen.

Broken Relationship Journey

I realized I tend to bring all my childhood feelings into my adulthood. Relationships have always been hard for me because I did not know how to express my feelings and my needs. It was only after going through training and learning positive self-talk and affirmation that I was able to start seeing me as someone worth loving. I would start to routinely do self-talk and affirming myself. I became so proud of who I am and felt confident in my future. I started to see myself as a role model for teens; this is something I never thought I would be able to do.

I remember feeling ready to enter a long-term relationship and possibly marriage and I prayed about it. I had relationships that did not go far. Many times, I think it was because of how I was-Very closed in, allowing things to just happen and never really expressing what I expected from the relationship. I wanted so much to have a relationship that I truly felt safe to share my thoughts. So, I felt ready when I met the person I thought was "Mr. Right." I felt so sure at the time this was the person that was meant for me. Everything at the time felt right.

I remember checking off all the things that I wanted to know about this person and the rules of being a Christian woman entering a relationship that leads to marriage. No, I wasn't perfect; some lines were crossed during the dating period. But I tried my best and I prayed and felt God heard my prayers. I wanted so much for things to be done right.

The proposal was at Coney Island. He was so nervous. I went straight into planning the wedding and the wedding day. Everything felt right. I felt like the little girl inside me had grown up now. I felt confident I was now able to express my needs and expectations to this person. My health struggles I made sure he was aware of, especially to the fact that it will take a miracle for me to provide him with a child. I was so nervous I would be rejected by him on that, but it seemed to be alright with him. So, we got married. I wish I could say we lived happily ever after and married life had been a fairytale. Brokenness started to set in the marriage and the relationship is now toxic.

When this part of my journey was hit again with overwhelming circumstances, I had no choice but to look at the person in the mirror. The person I saw was a person that was broken and I thought I could not be put back together again. I was at a place on my journey in my story where my heart had been broken again; pain and disappointment had taken over. Shame and pride were now becoming my friend. I was shattered, and I cried out to God for help; but he seemed far.

I thought I was on the road of reconciliation and restoration in my marriage. I forgave the betrayal and came to terms with a child bornin the marriage that is not mine. I thought this time I would have my miracle child. It happened at a time when I felt spiritually connected to God. I had just completed three years of study at Bible school and had graduated top of my class. I was now getting over allowing procrastination to control my life. I felt ready to step into the next level. I forgave him But I found myself shattered in the midst of it all. *What did I miss*, I asked myself. All the childhood feelings of self-doubt, low self-esteem came right back hitting me in the face. This revelation came to me:

"I am standing in my current story but it is only one point of my journey, one chapter of my journey. Yes, this point of my story is painful. These pages are full of hurt but this is my journey and it does not end here. My current story is emotionally and physically painful. How could I open the door to him again, I asked? What was I thinking? Did I not see that this would happen again? Why did I put myself, my heart through this again? All I knew at the time was that I wanted to do the right thing and try again on the marriage road. God, you have forgiven me, I said to myself, then I should forgive too. How would I know I was going to be hurt again? With all of that, here I go again with reproductive issues.

Another surgery is what I must face. And no child to show for the pain I suffer. I tried to accept that maybe I wasn't meant to have children but something keep saying, don't give up. He is back so now I thought we can try again to have a child. I am so tired of the circle in my life. This is too painful; this is my story. I must now accept this phase of the journey. I must own it. I cannot wash it away, I cannot hide from it. It is a part of me and who I am.

Revealed to be Healed   Paula Carroll

This present time is a part of owning this point of the journey and realizing the realness of it. It is painful; the hurt is there. It is fearful, I am scared. It is disappointing, and the shame is there. I must admit, a part of me wants to roll up and die. A part of me does not want to face it or own it. I did not want to own divorce as a choice. I wish I could erase it all. Yes, all I want to do is erase it and start all over again as if this had not happened. But it is my story; it is me. I must now get up and face the giant. The giant is me. I must now face me. This is me. This is my story.

I realize the journey must go on. I cannot stay at this point; I cannot rest in this chapter. I must not allow the pain, the hurt, the fear, the disappointment and shame to keep me here. But, how do I move on? How do I get out of these pages of my life? How do I get beyond what others will say? How do I feel whole again? The tears are falling; my eyes are heavy. My heart feels like it was shredded in pieces. My prayers feel unanswered. God, do you hear me? Do you see me? I am weak and tired. I don't want to fight any more.

I realize I have a weakness and that is getting in the way. I am like a person who is color blind. When the light is red, signaling to stop, I see green and I go. I listen to the wrong voice. I allow underlying desires to overtake reality. I open a door that should have been kept shut.

Do I have what it takes to move on, to take the steps from this point to write the next chapter of my story? As the tears flow, I come to realize

I must own my story in order to move on. How can I own this story? How do I move to the next chapter? Do I have what it takes to own it and move on? This is me, this is my story. I must own it."

Owning it is accepting the past for what it is, accepting the present and live it. Accepting that a new story is ready to be written. The girl I was and the woman I have become is all a part of the journey and it is worth owning it. I read a quote that says, "The Struggle is part of the Story." There is no story without struggles and there is no journey without stories.

I come to understand that our journey will come to a pause at times; it will face challenges and trials on the way. It is how we move from that stage that is of importance. It will determine the next chapter of the journey. Owning my story is a way for me to move from the *why me*, the *how could it happen to me, it should not happen to me* and move to- *this is me, this is happening, this had happened to me, why not me*? Realizing I am one of many women this has happened to on the journey.

Struggles are part of the Story.

Stories are part of the Journey.

Own it!

Reflection

Where are you on your journey? What is your story? Take some time and reflect on some of the stories that make your journey. Use the space provided to write about a story on your journey that you had to own or are in the process of owning:

_____

_____

_____

_____

_____

_____

_____

_____

_____

_____

_____

_____

_____

Revealed to be Healed — Paula Carroll

Revealed to be Healed   Paula Carroll

Revealed to be Healed　　　　　　　　　Paula Carroll

What to Do to Move On

Owning it on the journey is a process. It may take some time to reach the place to release it. During the process of owning it, I had to do some self-check. Am I still self-blaming? Am I still angry with me and others involved? Did I let go of self-pity? Do the words, comments, and criticism still bother me?

People's opinion regarding the situation and where I am on the journey can be a setback or a motivator to move on. How I react and handle the opinions of others will determine how long the process of owning it will take. People in general have difficulty letting someone go. This is where your control of the situation is tested, when all the steps of the process are complete, and people still have not let it go.

Are people still holding me to that 15-year-old pregnant teen? Am I still looked at as a person without voice or am I held to the mistakes I made? God is the one who justifies us.

> Romans 3:23-24 *23 for all have sinned and fall short of the glory of God, 24 and all are justified freely by his grace through the redemption that came by Christ Jesus.*

Owning it is gaining the ability to not hold oneself to other people's expectation. When God opens the door, we must move and not be held back by the opinions of others. He will take care of us. People will hold you back if you allow them. Negative comments and criticism can pierce like a knife. Sometimes people come with good intentions but say the wrong thing. Job's wife and his friends are great examples of that.

> <u>Job 2:9 & Job 4:5-6) Job2</u>
>
> *9 His wife said to him, "Are you still maintaining your integrity? Curse God and die!"*
>
> <u>Job 4</u> *5 But now trouble comes to you, and you are discouraged; it strikes you, and you are dismayed.*
>
> *6 Should not your piety be your confidence and your blameless ways your hope?*

To own my story and accept where I am on the journey is a way of finding peace and power to stand. Instead of allowing myself to be consumed by anxiety, fears, and worry, I am set free. Free to accept that through it all God loves me, and I can express that love given to me. Owning it is experiencing the hurt and not denying what I am feeling. It's not saying I am Ok when deep down I am hurting. The hurt is real; the pain of hurt by someone, feeling disappointed and shameful is a reality and acting as if it doesn't matter is denying oneself the opportunity to heal.

Rick Warren wrote in his message *Connecting with God,* "Revealing your feeling is the beginning of healing."

Owning it is also getting the courage to reach out to the people placed in your life for helping you through the healing process. Having a network of sistas during this process provides the opportunity for strength building and safety to be honest.

> Rick Warren also wrote, *"When we don't have one person in our lives that we're completely honest with, we wear a mask. ...We pretend that we have it all together, when everybody knows we don't. We act like it's all right when it's not."*

God knew I needed to hear the voice of a friend. I needed a listening ear. I needed to be prayed for and prayed with. I realized that during the painful process of my story I needed someone and that is ok.

Connecting with other Sistas on the journey is vital to getting to the place of owning my story. God has placed some great sistas in my corner that I could call on. And even when pride did take over, they did not hesitate to reach out and let me know they were there if I needed them. One of these very sistas is a mentor God hand-picked just for me. Rev. Porter Cox. I did not have to call her. Through divine direction, she would reach out to me at the very moment I needed a sista friend.

Seeking God is key during the process of owning my story. There were days when I felt so weak, felt like giving up and only God was able to strengthen me and give me hope. In seeking God, I had to confess my true feelings. I may have been able to mask my true feelings from people but God could see my brokenness so it does not pay to hide from Him.

> Psalms34:17-18 *when the righteous cry for*

help, the Lord hears and delivers them out of all their troubles. ¹⁸ the Lord is near to the broken hearted and saves the crushed in spirit.

God knows just what to do to pick you up and put you on the path of complete healing. In seeking God, I find myself just crying, not able to put into words what I am feeling or need. But He knew everything about me so there was a time I would just open my mouth and just can't stop talking to Him. Another time I would find myself writing a letter to God. Whatever method I used, I know God heard them all. He is able to give me peace, strength and hope to own this story.

2 Timothy 1:7 *For God hath not given us the spirit of fear; but of power, and of love, and of a sound mind*

Owning it is also getting the courage to reach out to the people placed in your life for helping you through the healing process.

Owning my story on this journey is a process of resiliency. Owning my story is acknowledging that, despite the pain, the struggles, this is just one chapter of the story and this story is just one of the many stories on the journey. I embrace the pages of blessings, of joy, of peace as well as the pages of pain, of struggles, of trials on the journey. The journey is in the hand of God who is the author and finisher of the journey. I own my story and place it in the hands of God because he holds the original plan of the journey. Owning it is taking that step into the plan God created from the start of life. I am reminded in Jeremiah 29:11 that God has a plan for me and that the plan is good for me and it will not hurt me. The plan allows for prosperity and gives hope for the future.

Revealed to be Healed   Paula Carroll

The Stop Signs

Owning my story required me to self-check and analyze where I am and where I want to go. I now have to put up some STOP SIGNS in my life in order to move on.

❖ *Stop living for others and live for myself*

I have been a people pleaser since I was a child. I have this tendency to want to please everyone but me. I hold my feelings in to help someone else. Some may say, "oh, that is so nice." But it was killing me. I did not have a voice. I did not put *me* first before others so now I must stop living for others and live for me. God chose me and carved out a path for me so why am I wasting time walking a path made by others?

> *"For I know the plans I have for you," declares the Lord, "plans to prosper you and not to harm you, plans to give you hope and a future."*
>
> – Jeremiah 29:11

❖ *Stop thinking I owe anyone any explanation*

This goes hand in hand with being a people pleaser. Always thinking I must explain my life to others. Always thinking I must give people a reason why I do things in my life. Because of this, people start to expect this from me. In life, I make good and bad decisions. I make mistakes sometimes and that is ok. I now have to feel good about myself and the decisions I make and not have to explain myself to others. At the end of the day, it is me who I face. And as long as I am true to myself, then that should be enough.

> *"Being confident of this very thing, that he which hath begun a good work in you will perform [it] until the day of Jesus Christ."*
>
> - Philippians 1:6

❖ *Stop wanting to be right*

One of the hardest things for me to accept is that I was wrong. Being wrong for me means disappointing someone and I don't like to be looked at as one who did not do it right. Accepting my own weakness on the journey is a big lesson for me. I have now come to the realization that it is ok to not have the answer all the time, to not have to be right all the time. I am human and humans are imperfect.

> *"Therefore, I take pleasure in infirmities, in reproaches, in necessities, in persecutions, in distresses for Christ's sake: for when I am weak, then am I strong."*
>
> -2 Corinthians 12:10

❖ *Stop trying to be what I am not & Stop covering up pride*

My smile is two-fold. I smile a lot and realize how powerful my smile is. It is powerful because I use it two ways:

My smile is a greeter. I smile as I meet people and usually it is the first thing people see when they meet me. I also use it to cover up. I cover up pain and hurt. I walk around with a big smile when inside I'm dying and I don't want people to see. I pretend a lot and that is not the real me. I do try very hard to make sure people don't see the fragile side of me; the side that says, "I really need a hug right now. I really need some encouraging words and want someone to see I am in need." I many times allow pride to take the best of me and not reach out. No, I don't want to walk with my issues tagged on me but also don't want people to think I am this lucky-go-lucky-come person who has no needs to be met.

> *"Do not be conformed to this world, but be transformed by the renewal of your mind, that by testing you may discern what is the will of God, what is good and acceptable and perfect."*
>
> -Romans 12:2

❖ *Stop making excuses & Stop trying to fix it all*

Did I tell you I am one who likes to make things look good even when they are not? At one point I started to accept it as my duty to fix things. I try to fix all the wrongs, all the hurt. Yes! That is me, to the point where I will make all excuses and fix up for a person who I know is not doing right. I made excuses for the things I saw in my husband. I thought that would help him make the right decision. I made excuses for myself to justify the reasons I held on to something that deep down I knew I shouldn't be holding on to. This **STOP SIGN** is well needed for me to own my story and move on. I will **STOP** making excuses for others and be real about it.

> *"Be strong and courageous. Do not fear or be in dread of them, for it is the Lord your God who goes with you. He will not leave you or forsake you."*
>
> -Deuteronomy 31:6

- *Stop thinking I am not good enough, not strong enough*

I kept asking myself, how am I going to get out of this? How am I going to move from here? Do I even have it in me to make it beyond this? I know I don't deserve such pain, hurt, shame, and disappointment. My self-worth is on the line here. This relationship has me second guessing my value as a woman, my self-worth. Why am I not good enough for him? What is wrong with me, are the questions that plague my mind. I must remind myself of these words:

> *"....for I am fearfully and wonderfully made: marvellous are thy works; and that my soul knoweth right well."*
>
> - Psalm 139:14

- *Stop trying to live up to people's expectations*

For many years, I have lived or tried to live

according to what I thought others wanted of me, at least to some degree. The expectation of others will bring a person down, especially when it does not line up with what the person desires for themselves. This is a hard lesson for me to swallow but I must if I want to stay true to myself.

I remember my biggest disappointment to my family. That was when I got pregnant at fourteen years old. It is like from then I unconsciously decided that I will live according to how they want me to live and ever since then I have tried to fit into people's mind frame of who they think I am and who I should be. As I grew closer to God and saw Him as my creator, I started to see that the only expectation I should be living up to is His. Life lived by others expectation is not a life worth living.

> *"The LORD will work out his plans for my life–for your faithful love, O LORD, endures forever. Don't abandon me, for you made me."*
>
> -Psalm 138:8

Living up to the expectation of others or not to is the question. On your journey, you will come to the realization that some of the trials we face are connected to how we view and try to live out the expectation of others. On the journey of owning our story, we sometimes hold our **Self** hostage because of what we think people expect of us. During this process, we are finding ourselves and having to separate our self from the expectations of others, an enlightening or struggle can surface. We may be enlightened, realizing our own expectation and living up to it or we struggle with figuring out our own expectation while living in others' expectation of us. When we find our true **Self**, we find our voice, our own idea and give ourselves credit. This put us in the position of owning our story and choosing our own terms of how to use our story in whatever fashion, we choose. In other words, you now have choices and get to make that choice.

I will run the race God set before me. I will continue to run to him my savior. I may not like this part of my story but my journey continues. God is with me and I need not be afraid. Amen

---

And you thought it all happened to break you.

Instead you stand tall and say,

STOP SIGN

Ahead

Reflection

What are your STOP SIGNS? Take some time and reflect on some of the STOP SIGNS you had to put up to move on to your next chapter. Write a list of your stop signs:

_____

_____

_____

_____

_____

_____

_____

_____

_____

_____

_____

_____

_____

Revealed to be Healed — Paula Carroll

Revealed to be Healed — Paula Carroll

Revealed to be Healed — Paula Carroll

Accept the Following to Move On

DISCOVERY OF "I AM"

These are what I rediscovered about myself as I own my story and prepare myself to move on to the next chapter of my life:

- **I am** a strong black woman
- **I am** a woman of strength
- **I am** a child of God
- **I am** worth loving
- **I am** my own person
- **I am** valuable

Sometimes that is all it takes.

Rediscover your I AM

Revealed to be Healed

Paula Carroll

Reflection

Take some time and reflect on your "I AM"

I am:

Revealed to be Healed   Paula Carroll

Revealed to be Healed

Paula Carroll

Revealed to be Healed

Paula Carroll

Release It

Owning my story is just one phase. The next step is releasing it. Release means to let go. I must release it to gain back control and start the new chapter of the journey. As I mentioned before, in the process of owning it, these questions are asked: why me? How could it? But I must move from that stage. I have come to know that my journey makes me who I am, so I can't just erase part of who I am. I can set myself free from staying there. Releasing it is finding peace; it is feeling free from the bondage of being stuck there. Releasing it is realizing that I am no longer controlled by what happened. It is taking control of myself and moving forward.

Moving forward is to take the first step: starting that new chapter of my journey. I release it so the bond of sistahood and praying sistas can carry me through. Release it so I can be whole. Releasing is saying, "No more pity party. No more, "how could it happen to me?" Releasing it means I stand tall and in control. It is being able to tell my story without fear, regret, and shame. When I release it, it opens the door to healing. Healing from the pain the hurt the shame, and disappointment. It is a sign of liberation, freedom, and redemption.

> Isaiah 43:1 *"...Do not be afraid, because I've redeemed you. I've called you by name; you are mine."*

I was able to give myself permission to give

and receive love when I release. I now find strength in my story.

Releasing it is to become unashamed of what makes your story what it is. Unashamed that you too have a story. One of my favorite sayings is, "Everybody has a story." Without a story, there is no journey.

Being a Jamaican, I come from a culture that teaches from early that, "you don't hang your dirty laundry in public." With that lesson, we learned from early how to celebrate outwardly success and great accomplishment but cover up pain, shame, guilt, hurt, and disappointment. We became good at pretending, holding our pain inside, not knowing how to reach out and seek help, not having a voice. When you Own it and release it you now feel free to share it if you choose. The cultural barriers, cultural norms are broken and now you are unashamed and unapologetic of your story. Being unashamed is understanding that the journey continues, and another story now can emerge. God is still working it all out; he is preparing you for the next chapter of the journey.

So, while I can say, "I have overcome that. I now own that," there is still more to do, the journey continues, and I need not to be ashamed. Releasing my story helped me to see that I am able to stand strong. I am able to rise above my circumstances and recognize that I am the daughter of the Most High. I am blessed and highly favored. I am loved and valued.

> Isaiah 16:10 *I delight greatly in the Lord. My soul rejoices in my God, for he has clothed me.*

Releasing it is allowing for the process of forgiveness. Forgiveness is the process of letting go. Forgiveness opens the doors to healing, feeling free from the control of the situation or person over your life and allowing for an understanding of the story. Forgiveness does not promise forgetfulness. But it can bring a sense of peace that gives way to moving on. There is no doubt that future experiences will trigger memories of past hurt and struggles. It is when you allow the process of forgiveness to happen that you will be able to return to that memory and feel a sense of peace with that story.

Forgiving of self and others is the form of releasing the story you are in. You may say, "forgiving someone I can understand, but why do I need to forgive myself?" Forgiving oneself is a vital part of the forgiveness process. Many times the story we have experienced left unnoticeable scars. We beat up on our self and find it hard to move beyond because we have allowed what has happened to us to define us. Forgiveness gives courage and when we forgive self we gain courage. Courage to stand bold, stand tall, and release. It is like climbing to a mountain top and breathing in the fresh air; but the best part is breathing out and feeling the air releasing from our body, oh, so relaxed and free. Yes, your story is a part of who you are but it does not define who you are. Forgive others but, most of all, forgive **Self**.

It is when you allow the process of forgiveness to happen that you will be able to return to that memory and feel a sense of peace with that story.

Releasing my story is coming to the acknowledgment of my brokenness and the need for a higher power to take over. I was broken but not crushed, shaken but not crumbled, fell but I got up. I can now find peace in my story and a sense of freedom. I have come to the realization that true peace and freedom comes when I can no longer rely on my own strength but surrendering and releasing my brokenness into the hands of the Most High. During the process of owning it, I had to come to terms with the reality of being broken and, in releasing it, I can now feel a sense of peace, knowing that God's power is now in control. Out of the brokenness of my story, I reach out to God seeking peace and freedom to move on. No, Life did not just automatically switch to perfection, but because I now know that there is Power that is greater, I am now able to let go and release.

> Psalm 119:45 45 *I will walk about in freedom, for I have sought out your precepts.*

I know in the ears of others, your story sounds crazy, unbelievable, out of the norm. How do I know this? Because I too felt that way about my story. I heard the Spirit of God telling me, "this story you are in is not yours. You need to own it. You need to release it and watch how I, God, will use it." Many of us are not healed and even refuse to go through the process of healing because we are afraid. Afraid of what others will say when we share our story. Afraid to own the pain, the hurt, the disappointment of our story. Afraid to release it all. Afraid to step out of the current story and write a new one. We are just Afraid.

The story you are in right now will come to an end; that chapter will be complete and another story will start. The next chapter of your life will have stories that carry their own trials and struggles to overcome and own. In releasing the current story, you will see that God gives you the strength, teaches you the lessons, grants you the opportunities to release and for it to be used in the next chapter of the journey. Remember, God is still working on us in each chapter of the Journey.

> Isaiah 40:29 *He gives strength to the weary and increases the power of the weak.*

God gives us the ability to make choices. On this journey of life, I must make choices and when I reach that one spot on the journey where circumstance hit me as if to knock me out, I stop and own it, own where I am and then make a choice. I had a choice to hold on to it or release it, so I can move to the next chapter of my journey. The chapters I choose to release I can now use to propel, empower, and motivate myself and other sistas on their journey.

God can bring us to the next level of our journey when we release it all to Him. He will renew us, revive us, and restore us. We cannot use our story until we are fully restored. God is the strength of my life. In His POWER I can release it. In His POWER my journey goes on. In His POWER a new chapter begins. God's words said, "trial comes to make you strong."

I Release it, so He can use it.

I Release it, so He can use me.

I Release it, so He can empower me.

God's righteous right hand is strong; it will hold me up on the journey.

This is a new beginning, Lord. I place my future in God's hand, knowing that he has a plan for me and what you started, Lord, I know you will finish. Amen

---

And I will walk at liberty; for I seek thy precepts.

Psalm 119:45

Reflection

Use this space to write about how you can release your story and how it can be used.

Revealed to be Healed   Paula Carroll

Revealed to be Healed						Paula Carroll

Revealed to be Healed — Paula Carroll

Using It

On my journey, I met sistas who experienced similar circumstances on their journey. I met sistas who were able to move along and were restored. I met sistas who had different stories but were able to show strength. I also met sistas who were struggling on their journey. I realize I can find strength and be of strength to other sistas on their journey. Sistas are linking and connecting on the journey to form a solid foundation of power and motivation.

This is where my story can be used for the greater good. The word of God said, *the stone the builder refuses shall become the cornerstone.* Each journey is uniquely linked. Releasing my journey to God allows for God to work in me and through me to help someone else. Even though that chapter on the journey made me feel hurt, gave me pain, made me feel fearful, disappointed and even ashamed, there is purpose for it all. I now see that my life is purposeful and everything in it has a purpose.

No, I could not see the purpose at those times; I could not see where it was bringing me. Honestly, I thought it came to destroy, to take away my hope; but God had a plan for me. His plan for me was established from the time He created the first human and when He created me. God is not surprised by my story because He said, "I have a plan for you. A plan of good. A plan that will give you hope and a future." I can now use my story to get back to the original plan, the plan that was established by God, which is the main purpose of me being alive and living this journey. I believe that using it put me at the place to live out the plan and purpose God intended for me. My journey is now ready to be used to reach other women. I now see that this journey I am on is not just for me but a channel for God to use me to reach others. It is my belief that launching Sistas Journey is the vehicle that God allows me to walk in my **Purpose** on the journey.

I now see myself as a woman of God, living by Grace. As I journeyed in life, I have had the opportunity of having women who motivate and inspire me to be who I am today. No matter how difficult life got for me on my journey, God always placed a woman or group of women to help me along the journey. I would not be the person I am today if I did not have this network of women in my life, touching a part of my journey one way or another.

SISTAS JOURNEY was birthed out of attending a women's seminar at Blue Hills Church of God, now Rehoboth Church of God, on *Journey to the Well*, a book written by Vashti M. Mackenzie. It was there that I wrote in my notebook some 10 years ago, "well women, sistas journey, women group." Ever since then, I could not stop thinking about working with girls and women around transformation. God has reminded me over the years of what I wrote in my notebook, but I kept putting it off. My journey has been long and still going and I have expanded my women's network. But I always have the desire to reach out and connect women. I have come to learn that what God plants in you will grow and produce one day. SISTAS JOURNEY is what God planted in me and I am thankful that today I can say it is time to bring forth fruit. I look forward to the many girls and women's lives that will be touched and transformed through SISTAS JOURNEY.

SISTAS JOURNEY is an opportunity for women to use their own life's journey to support, inspire, provide service with thankfulness, advocate for a cause and reach their own self-awareness in a supportive environment.

SISTAS JOURNEY is about women of all walks of life, young and old, coming together to be a support to each other, through inspiration, service, thankfulness to God, self and others, advocating and reaching self-awareness individually and as a group.

When I think of **Owning it**, **Releasing it** and **Using it**, the process of a caterpillar transforming into a butterfly comes to mind. It symbolizes **New Beginning**, an opportunity to start new, fresh. It is shedding the old and stepping into a newness of life.

The butterfly was once a caterpillar and then entered into a cocoon. The cocoon represents the story on the Journey. As a butterfly, it had to shed the old and now step into a new way of living. Like the butterfly, we are able to own the story (cocoon), release it to the power of

God to take us through the process and allow it to be used. A butterfly will never return to caterpillar state. So the same way we will not be able to go back to the years before. We need not go back to the story we have just released. We now look forward to the beauty that emerges from the story. When we are changed from a life of brokenness to a life of purpose, we are not to go back to that story, that cocoon state. Newness of life is what we get when we are able to own the stories of our life, release it and allow it to be used and be of inspiration to self and others.

The butterfly moves around in the cocoon, ready to emerge into a new way of life. It pushes and the cocoon opens and it is at that time that life for the butterfly begins. It takes its first breath as a butterfly and opens its wings, ready to live a life full and free. The story of your journey allows you to push forth even though it was painful, hurtful, and shameful, had some disappointments. You are now a new kind of beauty.

The butterfly you have now become is like breathing life of newness, fresh start, new beginning. A new chapter of your life now begins.

You can't stay in the story.

That pain you had to endure means

change is happening

Revealed to be Healed   Paula Carroll

Reflection

Use this space to write about how you can release your story and how it can be used.

Revealed to be Healed — Paula Carroll

Revealed to be Healed — Paula Carroll

Revealed to be Healed — Paula Carroll

ABOUT THE AUTHOR

Paula Carroll is the founder of SISTAS JOURNEY and Co-author of *Soaring into Greatness*.

SISTAS JOURNEY is about women on a journey to transform and strengthen the Network of Life through Support, Inspiration, Self-awareness, Thankfulness, Advocacy, and Service. The mission of SISTAS JOURNEY is to empower women and young ladies in strength building and leadership development to overcome obstacles.

Paula Carroll is a case manager working with youth and family in the District of Columbia. She earned her Bachelor of Arts degree in Psychology from the University of Hartford, Connecticut and has been working in the Social Service field with a focus on Positive Youth Development for over 16 years. She has experience working with children, youth and families in various nonprofit agencies, schools and school based organization serving at risk youth and family. Her work experience includes public presentations, curriculum implementation, coordinating programs and Social Emotional Development coaching. Paula Carroll is also a youth leader in her local church and is a graduate of the Ebenezer church of God Bible Institute.

Paula's aim is to use her story on her journey in life of having the opportunity to have women who motivate and inspire her as a vehicle in reaching other women on their journey. She looks forward to the many girls and women lives that will be touched and transformed through SISTAS JOURNEY.

Revealed to be Healed   Paula Carroll